The Daily Telegraph

NATURE NOTES

The Daily Telegraph

NATURE
NOTES

ROBERT BURTON

Illustrations by
Michael Woods

Hodder & Stoughton

Text Copyright © 1998 by Robert Burton
Pictures Copyright © 1998 Michael Woods

The right of Robert Burton to be identified as the Author
of the Work has been asserted by him in accordance with
the Copyright, Designs and Patents Act 1988.

First published in Great Britain in 1998
by Hodder & Stoughton
A division of Hodder Headline PLC
10 9 8 7 6 5 4 3 2 1

A CIP catalogue record for this title is available from
the British Library

ISBN 0 340 728841

Designed by Behram Kapadia

Printed and bound in Great Britain by
Mackays of Chatham PLC, Chatham, Kent

Hodder and Stoughton
A division of Hodder Headline PLC
338 Euston Road
London NW1 3BH

Contents

Introduction

On April 3, 1949, my father, Dr Maurice Burton, met the editor of *The Daily Telegraph* to discuss a short weekly article on natural history. Four days later, the first Nature Notes (they were originally in the plural) appeared on the back page of the Saturday issue. On December 2, 1989, forty years and over 2,000 Saturdays later my father, by then in his 92nd year, reluctantly handed over the feature to me to follow in his footsteps. It was my life-long ambition to succeed him and use the column to express my own fascination with nature. I had started young. When I was twelve years old, I had earned a half-crown postal order for a letter published in the long-defunct *Junior Daily Telegraph*.

In 1949, nature study was still considered a rather eccentric subject for adults. It was not easy to admit to an interest in bird-watching, botany or bug-hunting. Even 20 years later, a friend enquired what I was doing on the bank of a stream. Rather than admit to watching sticklebacks courting, I replied feebly that I was doing nothing. Since those days, there has been a phenomenal rise in the appreciation of natural history.

Nowadays I find that, more often than not, people will be interested to learn about the courtship of sticklebacks or that I have siskins feeding on my peanuts and newts breeding in my pond. They will tell me what they have seen in their gardens and probably ask me to explain their own observations. This is the basis of Nature Notes: a simple anecdote of natural history followed by its interpretation. It is not always easy. We are still ignorant of many details of the private lives of even common animals. But, as part of the new public interest in natural history that has developed over the last half-century, there has been an upsurge in the scientific study of natural history. Ornithologists are now subjecting even the antics of birds in gardens to detailed scrutiny. This makes wildlife-watching so much more interesting.

For instance, I enjoy watching a skylark as it ascends on winnowing wings, singing as it goes, until it is a speck in the sky. The poet Percy Bysshe Shelley regarded the skylark as a symbol of freedom, and we earthbound mortals can certainly envy its freedom of the air, but it adds to my enjoyment to know that its blithe spirit is assisted by unusually well-developed flight-muscles. They confer on the skylark the ability to climb and hover, while pouring out the continuous song, and have the added value of enabling the skylark to escape birds-of-prey by out-climbing them. I read about this in a scientific journal and, for me, the dry objective account by the ornithologist is as exciting as the subjective rapture of the poet. And I can share it through a Nature Note with *Daily Telegraph* readers, so that the next time they walk through the fields and hear a skylark, they will benefit from knowing this little nugget of science that I dug out of academic obscurity.

Finding a new subject every week has never been difficult. I grew up with Nature Notes. They were a part of family life. When we saw something interesting, we would ask 'Daddy, is this a Nature Note?' in the hope that he would write it up. But simple observation is not enough, as I later found many years later when I first tried writing the feature. Under the critical eye of my father, I learned to be curious and look for explanations of the everyday activities of the most commonplace animals. There may be books in the running brooks and sermons in stones but there is immense fascination to be derived from understanding aphids on a leaf or sparrows in the street. I may be unique in having served an apprenticeship as a wildlife writer and I count myself lucky to have learned from a master.

My involvement with Nature Notes does not finish with publication on Saturday. One of the delights is to receive letters from readers. Their observations and questions raised may be ploughed back into another Note. Apparently simple questions are often extremely challenging to answer. When a reader described seeing a blackcap feeding on the stamens of mahonia flowers, I could not find any other record of this and reported the observation in a Nature Note. The result was 36 letters which added considerably to our knowledge of the relationship between a common garden shrub and visiting birds.

Scientific studies of our wildlife reveal fascinating details of the lives of animals but there is a drawback. After I had written about the antics of 'Mad March Hares', my fellow Weekend columnist Robin Page complained that I was 'demythologising' nature. The problem with science is that its more accurate picture of the natural world can appear dull and prosaic. I do not think this is the case because the pleasure of watching animals is not diminished in the least. For me, the attraction of science is that it reveals a world that is richer than I imagined, at the same time there is a delight in finding out how it is ordered.

Before the scientists started their patient inquiries into the habits of common animals, the countryside was full of marvellous tales of magpies' weddings, badgers' funerals, rooks' parliaments, rats carrying eggs, hedgehogs milking cows and other wonders. I fancy that Robin Page's real complaint against scientists is that the fox is no longer the romantic and mythical Reynard.

Understanding the behaviour of animals is a challenge. We cannot ask them why they do things. We can only infer from careful observations and check our hunches with systematic experiments.

But a perennial problem for the student of behaviour is that animals are not automatons. They are individuals whose conduct is not always predictable. Descriptions of a species' habits have to be peppered with qualifications such as 'seems', 'appears' or 'usually'. If I state categorically that an animal always behaves in a certain way or that some phenomenon never occurs, I am courting a adverse comments backed by eye-witness accounts that give the lie to my original confident statement.

Readers frequently enquire about strange behaviour that they have witnessed: a mole dustbathing, cats making friends with foxes, birds mourning dead mates. Even when I have discussed the matter with scientist friends, many of these letters are difficult to answer satisfactorily. These animals are not following the usual pattern of their species' behaviour and the only way to find an explanation for these unusual doings is to gather more eye-witness accounts until one gives a clue that hints to their meaning. With rare and unpredictable behaviour, this is well-nigh impossible.

One important wildlife subject that is seldom mentioned in Nature Notes is conservation. It is now almost impossible to write about any animal or plant without being aware either that it is in decline or faces threats to its safety. When I wrote about the water vole, I was well aware that the once familiar 'Ratty' has disappeared from many rivers and streams. A full discussion of the decline of the water vole would require more space than a Nature

Note can provide. Occasionally, however, a conservation problem is the trigger for a Nature Note. I once took a 20-mile walk along hedgerows and thickets in midsummer and failed to hear a single corn bunting. Its jangling song was once an inescapable part of the summer scene in my neighbourhood but this common farmland bird has declined drastically in recent years. This fact alone would not have made a Nature Note but I went on to say that I was unlikely to have missed singing males because their polygamous habits (a male with seven mates being the record) means they must sing frequently to keep their harems in order.

Great changes have taken place in the countryside since Nature Notes started. Countryside management has become more intensive. There has been loss of wildlife habitat as hedgerows, ponds and untilled corners have disappeared, meadows have been ploughed up, and rivers and streams straightened and cleaned. Woods have been felled and, on the other side of the coin, open habitats have been smothered with closely grown plantations of exotic conifers. The chemical revolution has produced powerful weedkillers and insecticides that have affected wildlife directly. And perhaps worst of all, enormous areas have been swamped by urban development. The result is that we are finding that animals and plants that were once abundant everywhere have become scarce or even rare. Ironically, at the same time there has been a surge of interest in natural history and great efforts are now made to preserve both the countryside and its inhabitants.

The Outdoors section of the *Weekend Telegraph* carries many conservation stories, and I have contributed to them, but the aim of Nature Notes is to stimulate the interest in natural history. If people are not interested in animals and perhaps not even aware of them, the conservation message will fall on deaf ears.

The Countryside Restoration Trust

In 1993, while I was wringing my hands over the disappearance of common animals and plants, Robin Page took the bull by the horns and set up the Countryside Restoration Trust. Why, he asked, should we have to travel miles to a nature reserve to see a barn owl or cowslips? They should be living in every rural parish. I was delighted when Robin invited me to become a trustee of the CRT. I was attracted by his insistence, as a farmer himself, that productive farming can be linked with attractive landscapes and plentiful wildlife. With the help of Daily Telegraph readers we bought our first 40 acres. Five years later we have 5,000 'Friends' and 235 acres of Cambridgeshire. Our ambitions are to spread our message and practical work by establishing CRT farms across the country.

For details, contact: The Countryside Restoration Trust, Barton, Cambridgeshire CB3 7AG.

JANUARY

Fieldfare

I t is said that the appeal of the robin is due to its big, round eyes. Large eyes are an attractive feature in our own kind, so it is not surprising that we find them so in other species. By contrast to the friendly, cheerful robin, a female blackbird has a sour look. The pale feathers under the bill give her a down-in-the-mouth expression. It is, of course, a mistake to transfer human attributes to animals, but it is difficult to resist the temptation and often gives a little harmless anthropomorphic amusement.

These thoughts came to mind when I turned my binoculars on to some fieldfares perched in the bare branches of an overgrown hedge. They looked as if they were frowning and I blamed this on the heavy black patch over the eye which gives them a knitted-brows expression. As it happened to be a cold, gloomy day, it was easy to imagine that the fieldfares looked as if they wished they were somewhere else, preferably much further south in the sunny Mediterranean.

Cold weather is not, in itself, a problem for birds or other warm-blooded animals. Providing they can get enough food to keep the inner furnace well stoked up to offset heat loss and maintain the warmth of vital organs, they will survive many degrees of frost. It is impossible, however, to know whether or not they feel cold and miserable as I do on a cold day, however well-fed I may be.

One of the sights I always stop to watch is a huge flock of starlings wheeling and streaming across the evening sky before settling into the roost for the night. Less familiar is the departure of the flocks in the morning. The starlings wake at dawn and start to chatter and bicker among themselves. The sky becomes brighter and suddenly there is a lull in the babble, as if a switch has been thrown. A few seconds later there is a resumption of the murmuration, as the starlings' chorus of twittering and whistling is called.

Bursts of sound alternate with periods of silence several times. Then, just as suddenly, a mass of starlings flies out of the roost in a dense cloud. The remaining birds resume their murmuration and a few minutes later there is another hush, and then another exodus of birds. The pattern continues until the roost is empty.

Waves of starlings fan out from the roost and spread over a radius of fifteen to twenty miles. In the reverse of the process, when the

flocks gather to go into the roost, they split up on their way out as groups drop out at feeding places while the main host passes on. Eventually, the dense mass of birds that clustered in the confines of the roost is dispersed over a huge area. It is believed that starlings that have not fared well the previous day follow birds that are heading off confidently, in the hope that they will be led to a better feeding place.

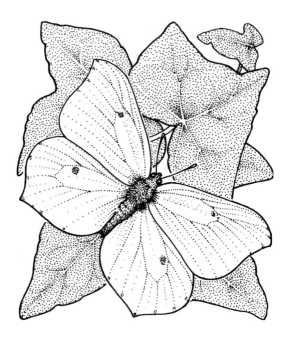

One of my ambitions is to find a hibernating brimstone. It is one of the butterflies that pass the winter as adults; others survive as chrysalises, caterpillars or eggs. Brimstones hide among evergreen foliage of ivy and holly, safe from chill winds and the hungry attentions of small birds, and they are difficult to find.

A hibernating butterfly has the same problems as a bat or hedgehog. It must enter its winter sleep with sufficient food reserves to sustain it until spring. Hibernation is probably induced by the shorter days and, initially, the butterfly will not wake up even in warm weather. After mid-winter, the embargo on reawakening is relaxed and brimstones, along with small tortoiseshells, may be seen on the wing on fine days.

This may be a heartening sign that winter is loosening its grip, but these early risers may be doomed. They are using up precious food reserves with little or no chance of replenishing them. But it may be that they are flying only far enough to find a more suitable hibernating place. If the current roost is getting too warm, the butterfly's body processes will speed up even while dormant and they may starve. It might then be worth looking for a more sheltered, cooler site. We have much to learn about the mysteries of butterfly hibernation, and it would help if the butterflies were easier to find.

S hould you consider making a pet of a garden snail, you could be taking on a long-term commitment. It might live for as much as ten years. On the other hand, if left to fend for itself in the wild, two years would be a good expectation of life, and for perhaps half that period it will be inert.

When the going is hard and the weather has become too dry in summer or too cold in winter, snails 'shut up shop'. They withdraw their soft, delicate bodies into their shells and close off the entrance with several layers of slime that harden to make an impermeable covering called an epiphragm.

A snail can survive in this state of almost suspended animation for a long time. There are stories of apparently empty snail shells on display in museum cabinets suddenly coming to life after many years.

At this time of year many snails have gone to ground, digging themselves into the soil or hiding under stones and logs. Others have sought refuge up trees or on the walls of houses.

It is not unusual to find clusters of snails that presumably have followed each others' trails to arrive at a common destination.

When spring comes the snails will gradually emerge and search for fresh greenery. The emergence is more dramatic in dry regions when a countryside bereft of snails begins to seethe with them at the first downpour. I once witnessed this in the south of France when a sudden thunderstorm brought out swarms of snails, followed by groups of Frenchmen intent on gleaning an easy harvest of delicacies.

FEBRUARY

Goldfinch

L ast year I had a single teasel growing in the garden. This year there is a forest of them, all offspring of the original plant. I had left the rosettes of teasels in the border last spring so that they could throw up their tall stems, flower and set seed. A mass of seed-heads would, I reasoned, act as a beacon for goldfinches. I have been proved right because small groups, never more than three or four, have been visiting the teasel clump since early autumn.

Goldfinches are one of our prettiest native birds, with their bold pattern of red, yellow, black and white. It is easy to see why this collective name is a charm. It may, however, refer to their song. According to *The Shorter Oxford English Dictionary*, an old definition of a charm was 'a blended noise, as of birds, school-children, et cetera'. This describes well the goldfinch's twittering song.

Teasels are very much the goldfinches' plant and crossbills are the only other bird that feeds on them. The seeds lie at the bases of long tubes protected by sharp bristles and only goldfinches and crossbills have beaks long and slender enough to pluck them out. It is not an easy job, however, and goldfinches are more likely to feed on the open seed-heads of thistles, dandelion and groundsel.

Growing teasels is not the only way to attract goldfinches into the garden. They are increasingly taking to feeding on peanuts. But it is worth growing teasels anyway because they make a good winter feature in their own right, especially when crusted with hoar-frost on a cold, bright morning.

As each wave broke, water surged up the beach and ran back, draining out of the sand and leaving it water-logged. A small flock of herring gulls straggled along the tide's edge, standing motionless as the water surged around their legs then busily searching about them as it retreated. Occasionally, one would dart at some morsel swept in by a wave. Others were behaving in a peculiar manner: marking time on one spot as if they were trying to keep warm, or perhaps trampling grapes.

This is called 'foot-paddling'. After each bout of 'paddling', a gull peers at the ground around its feet and sometimes pecks at something that it has discovered. It reminds me of a chicken scratching for grain.

It is believed that herring gulls, and a few other birds, use foot-paddling to lure or perhaps drive animals to the surface. A close watch revealed that the gulls were picking up sandeels that had been hiding in the wet sand. In meadows, herring gulls foot-paddle to bring earthworms to the surface. They are sometimes joined by lapwings, which paddle with one foot.

The theory is that foot-paddling on dry land mimics the vibrations set up by a tunnelling mole, which drives worms out of the soil in a panic, or the pattering of raindrops which lures worms to the surface. On a sandy beach, foot-paddling may fool the sandeels into thinking that a wave is rushing in and that it is safe to come out. However, this is only speculation.

I t sometimes happens that a glimpse of a bird from an unusual angle gives me a brief moment of excitement. Then I realise it is 'only' something quite ordinary.

A bright green and yellow bird swept into my field of vision and landed on the end of a branch. Was it something exotic, a parrot perhaps? No, it was a green woodpecker, but an interesting bird nevertheless. Our usual image of a woodpecker is a bird hopping up a tree trunk while hammering the wood to extract insect grubs. But the green woodpecker is rather different from other woodpeckers because its main food is ants.

My green woodpecker flew down and spent twenty minutes probing the ground. After it flew away I examined the spot and found that it had excavated a conical hole about two inches deep in the top of an ants' nest. It had been working in the same way as other woodpeckers but, instead of chiselling into hard wood, it had used its weaker bill to dig a hole in the soil. It had then pushed its long tongue deep into the ants' nest to lick up the adults and pupae. The tip of the tongue is capable of independent movement and is very sensitive to touch so it can be guided into the galleries of the ants' nest to locate the occupants. I visualise the woodpecker using its tongue in the same way as when I reach under the table with one arm to rummage blindly in search of a missing pen.

MARCH

Ant

A bright afternoon after many dull days tempted me to start digging in the garden. If nothing else, the exercise would keep me warm while I waited for the subject of my week's note to emerge.

Inspiration came in a clod of earth turned out by my spade: exposed on one face was a mass of ants several layers deep and three to four inches across. As the fresh air warmed them, a few of the ants started to move slowly and lethargically. Those still in the mass were

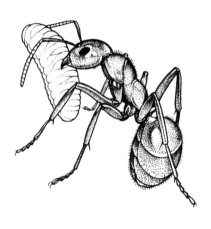

also stretching a leg or waving their antennae in slow motion to show that life was not extinct.

The more active ants began to wander about erratically but even in this semi-comatose state they found something useful to do.

To one side of the mass of ants was a patch of what looked like white eggs. Closer inspection revealed they were ant grubs, partly rolled up. Soon, each ant had picked up one of the grubs in its jaws and was walking around with it. The ants' instinct to look after the safety of the next generation is so strong that it was the first act for the rudely woken ants. Unfortunately, instinct did not tell the ants what to do with their burdens in the ruins of the nest.

All I could do was carefully replace the clod and hope that disturbance would be minimal if the ants quickly went back to sleep. It was better than leaving them to the tender mercies of the robin waiting nearby.

Pussy willow in full bloom, in sunlight, is a sight for sore eyes at the end of winter, the name perfectly describing the soft, furry appearance of the catkins of the goat willow or sallow.

The early flowering pussy willow supplies copious amounts of nectar to the first insects of spring. Even before the catkins are seen, the hum of hundreds of pairs of tiny wings can be heard on a bright day. There will be hoverflies, bluebottles and an assortment of small insects. Visiting butterflies include brimstones, small tortoiseshells and peacocks.

Newly emerged queen bumblebees lumber from twig to twig and feed furiously before starting to build their nests. Honeybee workers are attracted as they emerge from their winter coma. So are mining bees – solitary species of bee that can be mistaken for honeybees. Both sexes visit pussy willow, but only the females gather conspicuous bundles of yellow pollen for stocking the cells in their nest burrows.

Most catkin-bearing trees are pollinated by the wind but the willows are advocates of a belt-and-braces policy and employ both wind and insects for carrying pollen from male to female flowers.

In many parts of the country, pussy willow is called goose-and goslings, goose-chicks or simply goslings, in allusion to the fluffy yellow catkins. But it is more often known as palm, from its use in churches on Palm Sunday. Although not resembling palm fronds, sprays of pussy willow are a lovely substitute.

Hare

The antics of the Mad March Hare are part of our folklore and culture. More so than the gambolling of lambs or the crazy helter-skelter flights of lapwings, the headlong chases of hares across acres of fields are a symbol of supposed exuberance at the return of spring.

The maddest moment comes with two hares rearing up on hind legs and boxing each other with flailing paws. It used to be thought this was two bucks competing for the does' favours. However, while the bucks chase each other to determine their status, and pursuits may end in a fight with the teeth, the stand-up battles are between buck and doe.

The winner of the males' switchback chasing has the right to keep the doe company, but an overeager buck trying to impose himself on a less-than-eager doe is soundly boxed for his pains. He does not retaliate, but bides his time until her mood changes. He has to keep testing her because he cannot afford to let the moment pass. A bigger buck may arrive at any time and supplant him.

Although hare madness is connected with March, it is not confined to this month. It is most conspicuous at this time because more does are ready to breed and the hares' antics are conspicuous while the herbage and crops are still short.

I was surprised to receive so many letters about the derivation of the mistle thrush's name. I was reminded that the scientific name viscivorus means 'mistletoe-eater' and that the Roman writer Pliny started the idea that mistletoe berries would not germinate until they had passed through a mistle thrush's body. Mistletoe was used for making bird-lime, a sticky substance applied to branches to catch, for the pot, small birds that had the misfortune to perch on them. Combine the two themes and we get the Latin proverb 'Turdus sibi malum cacat', which translates politely as 'The thrush makes its own sorrow'.

The mistle thrush is one of those common birds that has a number of names. Some refer to its harsh, scolding notes: shrite and skrite, gawthrush and garthrush, jercock and syecock. But the best-known is stormcock. Bad weather dampens the activity of many birds but not the ebullient mistle thrush which will sing even through a snowstorm.

It is quite an experience to watch a storm-cock in the topmost limb of a tall tree, first tail-up then head-up as the gale bends the bare branches, and to hear its strident notes over the howl of the wind.

Yet another name is Jeremy Joy, apparently a corruption of January Joy, an allusion to the way the mistle thrush starts to sing at the beginning of the year.

APRIL

Tawny Owl

I was quietly nodding off in the bright sunshine after lunch when, among the mass of birdsong, I became aware that a tawny owl had hooted. The sound was enough to bring me out of my slumber and check whether I had been dreaming.

I hadn't. The full-blooded, quavering hoot of a male owl advertising its territory was repeated several more times. Tawny owls are the most nocturnal of our owls so these hoots were puzzling. I decided, as I relapsed into lethargy, that there was no particular significance to this behaviour. Diurnal birds occasionally wake up and utter a snatch of song from their night-time roosts, so there was no reason why the nocturnal tawny owl could not do the same by day.

But perhaps I am wrong in thinking that tawny owls are strictly nocturnal. It is true that they are beautifully adapted for hunting at night but they are not blind in daylight, as was once believed. My owl's mate will be sitting on their eggs and, when they have hatched, the pair will spend long hours hunting to supply the nestlings.

As the nestlings' appetites increase, but the nights grow shorter, the adult owls have to spend more time hunting by day to meet demand. It is not surprising that even a high level of diurnal hunting goes unnoticed. Tawny owls hunt mainly by sitting on a perch and dropping onto prey, but they will sit tight if they are disturbed by people wandering nearby.

A magnificent cock pheasant has taken up residence in the garden. He appears through the hedge and stalks across the lawn, the next best thing to having our own peacock. A few weeks previously, the garden had been invaded by a small flock of cock pheasants but they have now parcelled out the neighbourhood between them.

The pheasant's territory covers a large area and it maintains a presence by patrolling in a dignified procession of one, as P. G. Wodehouse put it. To reinforce the message, it joins the dawn chorus, uttering at intervals a loud, two-syllable crow, followed almost invariably by a whirring of vigorous wingbeats.

The pheasant's crow is audible to human ears over a mile so the much quieter wing-beating appears to be superfluous as a signal to rivals or prospective mates. Maybe the wingbeats create sounds that are too low for our ears but are audible over long range to other pheasants. This is known to be true for the American ruffed grouse.

Whatever the case, I hope our pheasant attracts some hens and we will be treated to the sight of him in full display: tail spread, body feathers fluffed out, ear-tufts raised and wattles inflated. I have invested in some extra birdfood in the hope that it will bring in the hens and we shall all benefit from the spectacle.

The planting of some new shrubs in a dry spell called for visits to the water butt to fill my watering can. The water, which had been clear all winter, was seething with tiny life. Small, pinhead creatures about one-sixteenth of an inch long were swimming jerkily through the top few inches of the water.

They were water fleas, so-called because of the way they hop jerkily through the water. They are propelled by the beating of two long

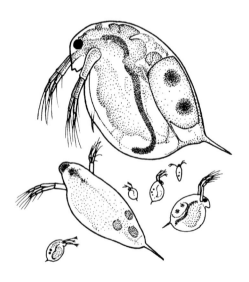

arms, which in fact are a pair of antennae. The net result of alternately swimming up and sinking back is that the water fleas gather at one level. They are sensitive to light and choose a depth where the intensity is not too much, not too little, but just right.

The water butt was installed last autumn, so where did the water fleas come from? The answer had to be down the drain pipe. During the summer, water fleas lay eggs which hatch into females without being fertilised. In times of drought or as it gets colder in autumn, some males are produced and they fertilise eggs which are laid in tough-walled packages that lie dormant until conditions improve. These were picked up in the plumage of birds that bathed in the shallows of the pond and were deposited on the roof of my house when they flew up there to dry and preen. From there the eggs were swept by the rain down the gutter and into the water butt.

This is the time when I hope to see my annual local wheatear. Since I have lived here, the odd bird has appeared every spring in the vast arable acres of sprouting winter cereals that surround the village. On this flat, open terrain, wheatears are easy to spot when they are disturbed and fly away from you. They flaunt the white rump that gave them their name, bowdlerised in Victorian times from the earthy Anglo-Saxon original.

These wheatears are on their way from winter quarters in Africa to their summer homes. Presumably, they will fly farther north when they leave my neighbourhood because nesting wheatears are rare in southern England. It has not always been so. A century ago, they were abundant over most of England but there has been a critical change of habitat in the south.

Wheatears are birds of short turf, which was once maintained in extensive swards by sheep and rabbits. They also relied on rabbit burrows for nesting places (I remember my amazement when I first saw a wheatear disappear down a hole). Their strongholds were the chalk Downs, the Cotswold and Chiltern hills, and the heaths of the East Anglian Brecklands.

Much of the short lowland grassland has disappeared and the wheatear is now typically an upland bird of the north and west of Britain, where rocky screes and drystone walls provide nesting places.

MAY

Water Vole

My introduction to the regularity of animals' lives came many years ago when the family spent a holiday at an idyllic watermill in Sussex. The river divided and flowed around the mill and we soon became familiar with the water voles that fed on the bankside and occasionally paddled across the stream. I soon discovered that they had regular feeding times because they came out as I was being called to our own meals. Observations had to be curtailed unless I could win special dispensation to leave the table early.

Water voles are the easiest small mammals to watch, apart from squirrels. They are more diurnal than most and they are easy to locate along river banks where their burrows, feeding 'lawns' and interlinking paths are very obvious. Poor eyesight makes them easy to watch at close quarters, but their hearing is sharp so you must approach cautiously.

It is rather strange that the water vole, moving 'feather-footed through the plashy fen' (as Evelyn Waugh's Boot had him in his column 'Lush Places'), has the scientific name *Arvicola terrestris* – 'earthbound field-dweller'. This refers to the habits of some continental water voles which burrow in pastures like moles.

Water voles are competent swimmers although they have few obvious adaptations for an aquatic life. They have flaps of skin to keep water out of the ears but, unlike water shrews, they do not have fringes of hairs on their toes to turn them into paddles or a 'keel' of hairs on the tail to make a rudder. Whereas water voles dive only to avoid capture, water shrews pursue their prey underwater.

The horse chestnuts on our village green are coming into flower and making a grand setting for the weekend cricket matches. At one time, coachloads of tourists heading for Cambridge would stop to take in this essentially English scene. Now they hurtle around the bypass — their loss, our gain.

In April the horse chestnut catches our attention with its sticky buds. When they burst, the leaves, each with five or seven leaflets on a long stalk, open out like umbrellas with extending handles. By the time the leaves are full grown, the candelabra flowerheads are ready to ripen. En masse, the effect is striking, but it requires a close look to notice the delicacy of colouring in each flower. There is a smudge of yellow that turns to crimson in the centre of the ring of white, frilly petals. The contrasting colour presumably acts as a target to guide the bumblebees that swarm around the flowers in search of nectar.

The game of cricket is part of the native scene but the horse chestnut is not. It was introduced from the mountains of south-east Europe and neighbouring parts of Asia late in the sixteenth century. Even now it is mostly seen in parks and avenues and does not flourish in woods. The name is something of a puzzle. It was once said that horse chestnuts were used for curing coughs and other diseases in horses. This was a back argument after the name had already been bestowed. The tree was probably named because it is inferior to the sweet chestnut.

My first contact with a cockchafer was quite painful. It hit me on the back of my head. I was walking through a grove of trees in a park when this large, solidly-built beetle flew into me. It was presumably as shaken by the incident as I was.

Cockchafers are often called maybugs from the month when they are on the wing. The first three years of life are spent as creamy-white, C-shaped grubs that live in the soil. They feed on roots and wreak havoc in grass-

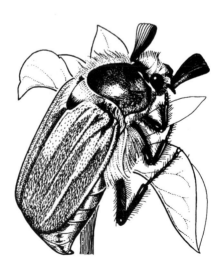

land and crops. On fine evenings, the adult beetles emerge, climb the stems of plants and take-off into the air. Their food is leaves of trees such as oak and lime.

Given their diet, it is not surprising that cockchafers are unpopular with farmers and foresters and that they are now not so abundant as they used to be. Before war was waged against them with insecticides, there used to be swarm years, when cockchafers appeared in enormous numbers. One naturalist described the buzz of their wings as sounding like the distant roll of drums, and the grinding of their jaws, as they chewed through leaves, like a saw cutting through hard wood. One unfortunate consequence of the destruction of cockchafers is the disappearance of the greater horseshoe bat. Cockchafers are one of its major food sources and their destruction has probably hastened the decline of a bat species that was never very common.

The swifts arrived suddenly, in the second week of May. We had had two days of cold windy weather, a heavy thunderstorm overnight and the next day was warm and clear. And there they were. I heard the familiar screams and looked up to see them circling high over the houses. They were intent on feeding on the insects that had emerged into the warm air and they would soon be starting to court and build their nests.

Swifts have a well-deserved reputation for being the most aerial of birds. They mate and even roost on the wing; their short legs make take-off from the ground difficult, though not impossible. Yet their name is surprisingly misleading. Their narrow swept-back wings and flickering wingbeats belie their speed. Reliable observations show that a swift flies at 12–20 miles per hour – more slowly than a house sparrow.

Of course, a bird that spends its life in the air must have economical, energy-saving flight as its priority, and this is achieved by not

hurrying. Moreover, it must be easier to spot and then pluck insects out of the air while moving slowly.

Swifts travel more rapidly when on migration and they undoubtedly fly very much faster when chasing each other, or when they are being chased by a hobby, the small falcon that hunts in flight.

June

Stickleback

The source of the Bourn Brook is one hundred yards down the road from where I live. During dry summers it virtually dries up but a small shoal of sticklebacks survives in the pool where the water bubbles out of the ground. These sticklebacks survive the depredations of village boys fishing for tiddlers but I have not found where they breed.

The easiest indication that breeding is taking place is the sight of a male, resplendent with red belly, guarding its nest of plant fibres on the stream bed. It refuses to move, despite severe disturbance. A clumsy swipe with a net sends it darting to safety but, within a few seconds, it is back on station.

Its success in life depends on defending the nest against other males and enticing females to lay their eggs in it. After the females have gone, the male stickleback continues to guard the nest and fan the eggs with its fins to aerate them.

Sticklebacks once existed in numbers that are hard to imagine today. The days are long past when a farmer could manure his land with sticklebacks. One farmer living two centuries ago on the banks of the River Welland paid a man to haul sticklebacks out at a rate of one halfpenny a bushel, and the man was said to have earned four shillings a day. Translated, this means he was catching 768 gallons or 3,500 litres of sticklebacks a day. What a bonanza such shoals of sticklebacks must have been for otters, kingfishers and herons.

I was surprised to see a mole scurrying along the bottom of a newly excavated drainage ditch. The ditch runs through the fields of a neighbouring farm and I have never seen any molehills there. I had concluded, sadly, that the place was devoid of moles, a species for which I have had a soft spot ever since I played Mouldiwarp the Mole in my school play nearly fifty years ago.

The mole was having difficulty getting out of the ditch. The excavator had left steep, smooth sides in the clay and the mole's spade-like front paws could not get a purchase. After falling back several times, it found a rougher section, scrambled up and promptly disappeared down a hole. I think it was luck that took it back into the security of its run so quickly.

The hole was three feet below the surface, which explains why I had not seen signs of moles in the fields. Once established, they do not spend their time excavating tunnels and heaving soil to the surface, but live at two or three levels in a network of tunnels which persist from year to year. They need to dispose of soil as molehills only during refurbishment and when making minor changes to the layout. The moles spend their time patrolling the tunnels in search of worms and insects that have fallen in. I suspect that my mole is living at a safe depth below the farming activities taking place over its head.

The heavy rain that followed the heatwave brought a previously unrecorded species into the garden: ducks, of course! A pair of mallards waddled up the lane, into the front garden and started to feed on the soaking lawn. They soon found the spot under the bird-table, usually favoured by collared doves and chaffinches, where other birds had wastefully scattered seed from the hopper.

The mallards were using rapid, dabbling bill movements to scoop up the seeds. When dabbling in water, a mallard uses its tongue as a piston to suck water into the mouth and drive it out again, trapping edible morsels on the row of transverse plates along the inner edges of the bill. It is a process that parallels the way whalebone whales sieve food from the sea with their baleen plates. This resemblance resulted in a pet mallard being christened 'Moby Duck'.

Nobody knows how the mallard sorts out the edible from inedible, but the tip of the bill is very sensitive to touch and it can locate hidden food by probing into mud or dense vegetation. Taste buds lining the palate and sides of the mouth — not on the tongue as in humans then help monitor palatability.

The rapid opening and closing of the bill in dabbling presumably functions as a mechanism for selective sifting, with the sense organs determining what is allowed through. This would explain why my garden mallards were dabbling even when there was no water to pump into the mouth.

JULY

Dragonfly

A cold spell in summer is not kind to insects. Only on warm days can I watch dragonflies at the pond. The antics of these superlative fliers alone are enough to make the pond worth its place in the garden.

When the summer sun does shine, there is usually at least one male circling the water with bouts of hovering and gliding to make itself conspicuous. The front and rear pairs of wings work independently, so you can hear them clattering as they flap out of synchrony. This arrangement gives the dragonfly immense manoeuvrability. It can hover, slip sideways, fly backwards or suddenly dart forwards faster than the eye can follow, wings beating together for maximum power.

Cold weather grounds dragonflies because their wing muscles do not work properly unless they are warm. Large dragonflies cannot fly unless the temperature of their muscles is thirty to forty degrees Centigrade,

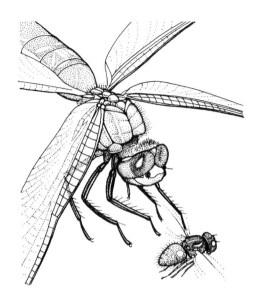

which is in the same range as the body temperature of warm-blooded animals. They warm up in the morning by basking, orientating their bodies to catch as much sun as possible, or by whirring their wings to generate heat by muscular activity. However, by noon on a baking-hot day, a large dragonfly on patrol can get overheated. So it flaps less and glides more to cut down heat production in its muscles, and uses its long abdomen as a radiator to cool its blood.

Once in a while, there is a good year for bee orchids. They turn up on roadside verges and patches of rough ground. In some places the plants are spotted soon enough for grass-cutting to be averted; elsewhere the orchids have to take their chance.

The flowers of the bee orchid and its relatives are famous for resembling various insects. The lip of a bee orchid flower looks like the abdomen of a bumblebee. In other species, such as the fly orchid, the resemblance

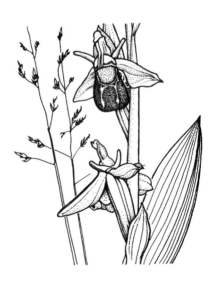

is part of a bizarre pollinating mechanism. Male insects are deceived into mistaking the flower for a female of their own species and attempt to mate with it. In the process, they pick up pollen which they deposit in the next flower that happens to trick them.

One wonders how such a bizarre mechanism could have evolved, especially as it does not seem to be very successful. Only very rarely have insects been seen visiting fly orchids, and they set very little seed. However, the bee orchid has dispensed with luring insects in favour of self-pollination. Bunches of pollen grains hang down and are trapped on the sticky stigma when the orchid is rattled by the wind.

The bee orchid is a particular delight to find because its occurrence is so uncertain. V. S. Summerhayes wrote, in *Wild Orchids of Britain*, of visiting a field where it was difficult to step without treading on a bee orchid. The following year, he could find only about a dozen plants.

I was taking my evening walk through the wood when I saw two large animals running ahead of me through tall vegetation bordering the ride. My first thought was that they were muntjac deer, which are a common sight here, but they were too squat and the colour was wrong. I was delighted to realise they were badgers because meeting badgers away from their sett in daylight is one of those serendipitous moments to be treasured.

I would have liked to follow these badgers but they ambled off through dense undergrowth where I could not follow. I wanted to know what they were finding to eat, because the ground was baked dry. Earth-worms make up over half the diet of badgers but they virtually disappear from the menu in dry weather when they are forced to burrow deep. A few weeks later, these badgers would have invaded the fields and ransacked the crops of wheat and barley but the ears had hardly begun to fill.

I suspect that the badgers were trawling the wood for anything edible. This would include small mammals – voles and mice, young hares and rabbits if they were lucky and unpalatable shrews if they were very hungry – birds and their eggs, and insects, such as beetles and various caterpillars and grubs. They may even have been forced to eat green plants to fill their bellies. Settled, dry weather is good for Wimbledon but it is a time of belt-tightening for some of our wildlife.

Swallows fly high in fine weather, and low when wet weather is on the way — was the first piece of natural history lore that I remember hearing. I later learned that the poet Thomas Gray — best known for his *Elergy in a Country Churchyard* — wrote:

When swallows fleet soar high and sport in air
He told us that the welkin would be clear.

Many years' observations have failed to convince me of the truth of this idea. The reasoning was that the weather affects the height at which the swallows' insect prey flies, but this is not completely borne out by the facts.

Wet weather restricts the activity of insects, especially the larger types such as hoverflies and bluebottles, which swallows prefer. These insects are likely to hide in vegetation or fly in the shelter of trees. Other kinds gather over stretches of water. So swallows will be seen flying low to hunt them and even pick them off leaves. Yet good weather does not change the altitude of the swallows' flight. They prefer to fly low in long, skimming sweeps across open ground in even the hottest spells. There is even a record of a cricketer catching a swallow, in mistake for a soundly struck ball.

Higher levels are usually left to martins and swifts, which prefer smaller insects. Warm, ascending air on a summer's day may be swarming with aphids or flying ants and sometimes swallows join the other birds in hunting them. So, there is some truth in the saying. But do not rely on it.

AUGUST

Butterwort

The flowers of butterworts are similar in form and colour to violets but the plants are immediately recognised by the rosette of fleshy, yellow-green leaves that lie on the ground like a stranded starfish. While violets are most often seen in woods and hedge banks, butterworts live on peaty moors, fens and heaths where the ground is fairly acid.

Butterworts have fascinated naturalists since Charles Darwin first demonstrated that they are carnivores. The upper surface of each leaf glistens with tiny droplets that make it a living flypaper. When an insect touches a droplet, it is drawn out and sets into a strong fetter. As the insect struggles, it is bound by more droplets. The leaf then secretes digestive fluids that dissolve the insect's flesh into a 'soup' which is absorbed into the plant's tissues.

The usual 'prey' are tiny flies and aphids but butterflies are sometimes caught. I have heard of a mountain pass looking as if a shower of snow had fallen after a cloud of white butter-flies had swarmed through on migration, leaving many of their number caught by a large colony of butterworts.

Like the sundews of boggy ground and bladderworts of peaty pools, the carnivorous habits of butterworts help the plants to thrive in an impoverished environment. They can survive without a 'meat meal', but flower more abundantly and set more seed if they get extra protein.

The verge between the ripening wheat and the road was only a few feet wide but it was a blaze of colour. For a while, often until they are cropped by a flail mower, it is possible to find stretches of roadside blossoming with the old flowers of arable fields. On this occasion, I noticed scarlet poppies, pink bindweed, blue cranesbills, white campions and chickweeds and yellow bedstraws. There must have been more but I was on a 'fun' run at the time and, although

sorely tempted, could not stop. What was in little doubt is that fifty years ago the fields I was running through would have been so much more colourful. It would have been a beautiful sight, except of course to someone earning a living by farming.

Many arable weeds are annuals. They are plants whose lifestyle is to germinate, flower and set seed within a short space of time. This allows them to thrive in arable farmland because they can shed their seeds before a field is harvested and the weeds are carried off with the crop. Another feature of these plants is that the seeds retain their viability for long periods.

Poppy seeds, for instance, will still germinate after eighty years or more of burial in the soil. As soon as weed killing is relaxed, poppies and other weeds stage a comeback. All they need is the soil to be disturbed. This may be through cultivation, construction of roadside verges or the upheaval that took place on the battlefields of Flanders.

Once in a while, bathing on our south-west coasts becomes less than inviting. The sea is invaded by fleets of Portuguese men-o'-war, which are jellyfish-like creatures armed with potent stings. They can produce a nasty weal on the bodies of bathers or on the hands of anyone handling them. Portuguese men-o'-war usually appear after persistent south-westerlies have blown them up from tropical seas.

The Portuguese man-o'-war is related to jellyfish and sea anemones but, like coral, each 'individual' is an indivisible colony of animals. One type forms the air-filled float, others are concerned with feeding, breeding and catching food. The long tentacles hanging below the float are covered with an array of stinging cells that stun fish as large as mackerel.

The origin of the name dates from the 15th century when the Portuguese were exploring the oceans in lightly-built, manoeuvrable ships called caravels. English sailors would have noted the similarity between the fore-and-aft lateen sails of the caravels and the floats of

Portuguese men-o'-war. The latter are twisted so that the animals drift at an angle to the wind like a ship sailing on a tack.

The Portuguese man-o'-war has one advantage over the caravel. When the sea gets rough, it deflates the float and sinks beneath the waves. When conditions improve, the float is pumped up again and the Portuguese man-o'-war drifts on its inexorable way.

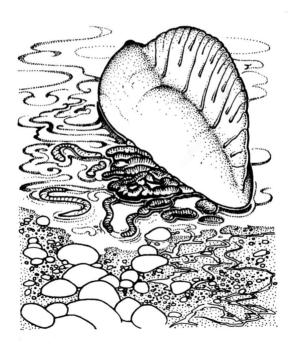

I had just remarked on the abundance of minnows and dace cruising below the surface, and how this showed that the brook's wildlife had survived after long stretches had dried up in the droughts of recent years. Would it be too much to hope, I wondered, that we might see the return of kingfishers or even otters? At that, there was a shrill call and we just had time to look downstream and catch sight of a brilliant blue streak disappearing around the bend.

Spotting a kingfisher is always a special occasion and this one was doubly welcome as a token of the brook's return to health. Usually the kingfisher is gone before we have time to exclaim on our luck. The real good fortune is to find a perch overhanging the water where the kingfisher can be watched launching lightning strikes against fish. When hunting, a kingfisher peers fixedly at the water below its perch with the intensity of a cat staring at a bird. Every few seconds it shifts its gaze, its beak pointing at a new angle. The dive is sudden and very direct as the kingfisher plunges without warning, but it may leave its perch and hover like a hummingbird, while lining up on its victim before powering head-long into the water. I was not surprised when I noticed that a kingfisher moves to a new perch after each dive. There is no point returning to the same perch after all the fish in range have been scared away.

W hen I lived in the western Highlands, forestry workers would casually remark that the midges had been 'awful bad' that day. I could not understand how they survived a job that not only stirred up the midges, but occupied both hands and hindered swatting.

The female Highland midge, like a mosquito, has a blood meal before laying her eggs. From the way that a cloud of midges gathers the moment you step out outdoors, blood meals would seem to be in short supply. Mammals and birds are alternative sources of blood but, if a midge cannot find a feed, she can still lay a few eggs.

The meal takes three or four minutes and, given the stinging sensation it imparts, it is rather suicidal. The body responds to the bite with a free flow of blood to the wound which brings up defences to combat possible infection and eventually clots to seal off the wound. The delay in clotting gives the midge plenty of drinking-up time. The itching and swelling that follow are no more than part of the body's normal repair mechanism, although this is no consolation when repairs are being effected all over your exposed flesh.

The cruellest part is that midges continue to bite when it is raining. If it is not bad enough that the grandeur of the mountains is obscured by falling water, it is worse that clouds of midges are trying to bite you. They prefer dim light, so they are particularly active in cloudy weather.

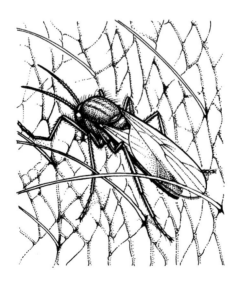

SEPTEMBER

Hermit Crab

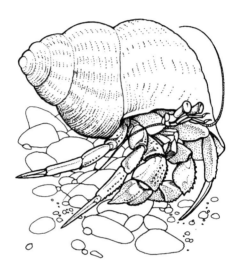

A hermit crab is always one of the prize finds in a rock pool. For some reason lost in the mists of antiquity, hermit crabs stopped making their own body armour and started to live in the shells of long-dead molluscs. This has necessitated a radical rearrangement of the body. A hermit crab is essentially a small lobster with a soft-skinned abdomen (twisted into spiral that fits into the shell).

As the hermit crab grows it has to move into a larger shell. Small individuals live in winkles, dog-whelks or topshells and full-grown ones graduate to whelk shells. When a hermit crab gets too large for its home, it looks for a bigger shell. It spends several minutes turning a suitable specimen over in its claws, carefully examining it until satisfied. The new shell must not be too small, or too large, but just right. A tight shell interferes with feeding and breeding while an overlarge one is difficult to carry. Having come to a decision and checked that the coast is clear, the hermit crab whips its body out of the old shell and quickly inserts itself into the new one.

If a hermit crab cannot find a suitable empty shell it turns bully and evicts one of its kind from its own shell. As they fight, the attacker assesses the size of the shell and, if not satisfied, it withdraws. If it has found what it wants, it grasps the shell and raps on it with its claws until the owner loses heart and moves out.

I had gone to the gravel pits in the hope of seeing hobbies, small falcons that find bodies of water attractive hunting grounds. As luck would have it, not a single hobby appeared but I noticed a swarm of whirligig beetles spinning on the water of the little bay where I was sitting. So I gave up ornithology and turned to entomology.

Whirligigs are amazing for the speed at which they swim and the way that they avoid colliding. The swarm behaves like dodgem cars which really do dodge rather than smash into each other (which I remember as being the greatest attraction of a visit to the fairground). In a burst of speed, a whirligig can reach 2.2 miles per hour. This does not sound much but it is two hundred body-lengths per second and twice the speed a house spider sprints across the carpet.

Collisions are avoided at this break-neck speed by a series of waves that travel ahead of the whirligig as it swims. These are registered by the antennae of other whirligigs, whose tips rest on the surface of the water, and avoiding action is taken. The antennae are sensitive enough for the whirligigs to distinguish between their fellows and other insects, such as flies, that have fallen onto the water. The ripples from their frantic struggles guide the carnivorous whirligigs to the hapless insects.

The spotted flycatcher is one of the small birds that seems to be on the way to losing its status as a 'common bird'. Certainly, it is a rarity around here. I had the opportunity recently to watch one in the garden when it stopped by on its migration south. Its fluttering flight as it sallied out from a perch, snapped up an insect and returned, immediately caught my attention. Other birds sometimes use this hunting technique but it is characteristic of the flycatchers.

At the limit of the sally, the flycatcher swings round abruptly and, for a split second, it can look like a large, grotesque butterfly. The tail spreads and divides into two halves so that there is a fleeting image of a bird with four wings. It was frustrating trying to observe this phenomenon but I got the impression of a bird that was hovering, tumbling, even looping in a skilled exhibition of stunt flying.

I wish I could have caught these aerobatics on film so that I could examine this split tail at leisure. It seems to me that it is a technique for increasing manoeuvrability at low speed.

Swallows and terns spread their forked tails to improve the airflow over the wings. By forming a slot behind the wing, air is sucked smoothly over the inner section of the wing to increase its lifting power when flying very slowly. Perhaps the spotted flycatcher is using its tail in the same way as it checks its flight and turns back to the perch.

A large, long-legged animal was creeping slowly on the ceiling. It was the time of the year when arachnophobes like me become edgy as outsize spiders invade the house. This particular creature failed to raise my hackles because it took only a split-second to register that it had just six legs and therefore was an unfrightening insect. It was a bush cricket with enormous whip-like antennae about three times the length of the body.

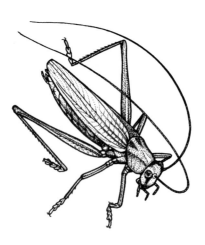

Bush crickets were formerly called long-horned grasshoppers, but they are more closely related to true crickets than to grasshoppers. Bush cricket is an appropriate name because they live in bushes, trees and hedgerows rather than in long grass. This preference makes them frequent inhabitants of rural gardens, although they often go unnoticed because they are well camouflaged and are active at night. The best time to find bush crickets is on summer evenings when the males 'sing' to attract females by rubbing their wings together. This one had been attracted indoors by the lights.

Perhaps the most surprising feature of the bush cricket is that, although it has the long hind legs typical of the grasshopper and cricket group of insects, it walks more often than it hops. This makes it very spider-like. Another apparent cause for concern among the faint-hearted is the long, curved 'sword' that looks like a fearsome sting but is merely the female's ovipositor for laying eggs in the soil or plant tissues.

O CTOBER

Water Shrew

T here was an outburst of squeaking where the cat had discovered something interesting in the flower bed. I went to investigate and found that it had brought a shrew to bay. It had reared up on its hind legs and was on the offensive – a veritable David challenging the Goliath of a cat.

I grabbed the shrew to save it from its tormentor and was immediately struck by its unusual appearance. It was bigger than a common shrew, as black as a mole above and distinctly white underneath. A closer look revealed tiny ears and eyes picked out in white. This was a water shrew.

Water shrews are semi-aquatic and sometimes live at a considerable distance from water. I have only once seen one swimming. It floated high in the water and then dived, turning from black to silver as its short, dense fur trapped a layer of air. The air presumably helps the tiny animal to keep warm in cold water but it also makes it so buoyant that dives last just a few seconds. This is long enough to pursue and catch freshwater crustaceans and insects, even small fish and amphibians.

I held the water shrew carefully because its bite may draw blood and inject a venom that leaves the skin sore and red for a few days. But it quickly escaped and, with a huge leap, landed in the pond. And that was the last I saw of it. It disappeared into a tangle of pondweed, where it remained submerged out of harm's way.

The hornet has a bad reputation. I doubt if many people have seen one and many fewer have suffered an attack, yet any large black-and-yellow striped insect is likely to be called a hornet and cause consternation. It may be the queen of a common wasp or even the very different woodboring wasp called a horntail. I have heard conflicting accounts of the ferocity of hornets. Sometimes they attack without warning or provocation but there are also stories of nests being disturbed and even wrecked without retaliation by aggrieved insects.

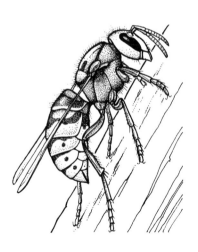

Discretion is certainly the better part of valour when encountering hornets and a friend had to stop going into the garden at night because of the hornets flying around the outside lights. She was surprised that the hornets should have been active as late as ten o'clock, at least two hours after sunset, when diurnal insects have retired.

Entomologists who collect moths by 'sugaring' – painting a tree trunk or fence post with treacle – have long known that the night-time catch sometimes includes hornets. Hornets have much larger eyes than other kinds of wasps and research has shown that they remain active at much lower light levels, to about the equivalent of bright moonlight.

In the autumn hornets join other wasps in feeding on ripe or rotting fruit. It is said that they get intoxicated on this diet and become the lager louts of the insect world, quickly turning nasty at any provocation.

For years I have made a pilgrimage some time during October or November to see the last of our wild flowers to bloom, the common ivy. My favourite site is a lone hawthorn growing in the middle of a field. It is burdened with a magnificent growth of ivy whose main stem rivals the trunk of the hawthorn for thickness. If the hawthorn were to be removed, the ivy would remain standing

on its own. When growing as a carpet on the ground or clinging to a tree trunk or wall, there are no flowers. Only when the top of the vertical surface is reached and branches grow free into the air does the ivy bloom.

The interest of ivy is its attraction to insects at this time of year because it is their main source of nectar. Other plants may still have a few flowers but ivy is unique for its late blossoming, beginning in September, reaching its height in October and often lasting well into November.

On a fine day there is an audible hum from the myriad flies and wasps gathering on the pallid green flowers to gather the nectar and pollen. In addition there are butterflies: tortoiseshells, red admirals, peacocks and commas. Many are newly emerged and have fresh, brilliant colours. At night a different shift of insects, including moths, takes over. For many of these insects death is imminent as winter approaches, but others exploit the ivy, laying down reserves of food for hibernation.

On fine evenings I watch for the black-headed gulls to appear. Within a space of a few minutes one hundred or so fly over the house, keeping to the line of the main road. They have come, I imagine, from a day spent foraging on the parks and playing fields of Cambridge and they are heading to roosts on the gravel pits.

The gulls fly in loose Vs, but with a few birds failing to keep in formation. Although difficult to prove, aerodynamic calculations show that flying in formation is a means of saving energy. The gulls are slipstreaming – flying in each other's wash to reduce the drag caused by their own movement through the air, and so minimising the energy needed to fly.

The formations look too ragged for this to work in practice. However, the calculations also show that the spacing between individual birds does not matter too much. They will get the most benefit if their wings overlap but the effect still works if they are further apart, and every little saving of energy helps when the gulls face a long, cold night.

The evening flight of gulls also reminds me of my childhood on the outskirts of London. Gulls heading up the Thames in the evening were a signal that my father would soon be home. This was not always true. My juvenile time-sense was not sufficiently developed to know that the gulls varied their departure from central London according to the time of sunset; my father was bound by the rigid timetable of the Civil Service.

Cranefly

There are craneflies everywhere. They are emerging from the lawn, shambling over the grass on their long, dangling legs and fluttering awkwardly into the air. They are floundering against the windows and settling untidily on the walls and ceilings. For many, their fate is to get entangled in spiders' webs.

Not many animals are total misfits but the cranefly is a good candidate. While its wings are about three-quarters of an inch long, its legs can be an unnecessary two inches and they are feeble organs of locomotion. The cranefly shares the nickname daddy-long-legs with the harvestman, a spindly-legged relative of the spider which is an agile and elegant walker.

The real life of the cranefly is spent below ground as a legless larva – the infamous leatherjacket which feeds on the roots and stems of grass, cereal crops, potatoes and other plants. It feeds through the autumn, winter and spring, and then pupates. The adults eventually emerge with one aim only in their short life – the establishing of the next generation.

The long legs of the cranefly appear to be a hindrance, but they reveal their function when the female lays her eggs. She inserts the ovipositor into a tiny crack in the ground, forcing it in by revolving the abdomen to and fro. During this operation, the body is poised almost vertically, suspended in a cradle formed by the legs.

A small hole in the ground, about one and a half inches across, could be the entrance to a mole's tunnels but, in the absence of further evidence in the form of molehills, it is more likely to be the work of a wood mouse.

If there is not a convenient shed or birdbox in the garden to provide a snug nesting place, wood mice live in burrows which are sometimes revealed by the spade, especially when

they form a network that has been occupied and enlarged by generations of mice. A single burrow system may extend over a couple of square yards and have several entrances.

A positive sign of occupation by wood mice is the blocking of the burrow entrance with leaves, twigs or stones. Rarely, the mouse – or mice because several may occupy a single burrow – builds a small cairn of pebbles over the hole. It may use pebbles up to half its own weight and the cairn is rebuilt if destroyed. We have to presume that this behaviour serves to disguise the entrance of the burrow or prevent a predator, such as a weasel, from entering.

Somewhere within the burrow, there will be a nest chamber, snugly lined with leaves or grass, and a separate food store. Seeds, conkers, fruit and berries, sometimes enough to fill a pint pot, are laboriously collected from a wide area. The mouse's labours may explain the mystery of disappearing sown peas or bulbs. One farmer found his field drains blocked by thousands of acorns.

NOVEMBER

Tit

I f you go down to the woods today, there is a very good chance that you will hear a chorus of piping notes coming down from the tree tops. They are the call notes of a flock of tits keeping in touch with each other. If you are in the right place, the chorus comes towards you and you will catch sight of the birds as they work their way through the foliage or flit from one tree to the next. Most of the birds will be blue tits and great tits, perhaps with coal and marsh tits or a group of long-tailed tits.

In an open wood, it is quite easy to keep up with the flock and hold the birds under observation as they industriously search for insects hiding in the bark and foliage. I followed a flock recently with the object of looking at the differences in foraging habits between the species. The most striking contrast is between blue and great tits. The former are very agile and are as happy upside-down as right-way-up. They are to be seen high in the trees, keeping to the outer reaches

of the branches and searching for food among
the leaves and twigs. Here they may be joined
by long-tailed tits. The heavier great tits,
together with marsh tits, prefer the trunk and
thick branches and also come to the ground.
The differences are not invariable but they
become apparent if you maintain watch for
long enough, and they are more marked when

One does not associate butterflies with Guy Fawkes Night. This is the day when we look forward to colours in noisier packages. But the autumn was so mild that there were red admirals in my garden during the afternoon of the fifth of November. There were hardly any flowers in bloom and the ivy, which is a mainstay for many late insects, was over although the rotten windfalls could have provided some nourishment. The red admirals were not interested, but one did settle on some dead leaves and sip droplets of dew.

I have never come across butterflies drinking water except when it is pond water providing essential salts. It is possible that something nutritious had dissolved into the dew from the leaves, but I doubt it. There would have been no time for the dissolving process to take place.

It is more likely that the red admiral was thirsty after a long flight. Butterflies seen late in the year are migrating and need to replace lost fluid. Red admirals seen in spring are most likely to have flown in from the Continent and their descendants, that appear in September and October, try to return home, although most, if not all, die on the way. Others hibernate, but their survival chances are slim and we owe our enjoyment of this gorgeous butterfly to cross-channel flights.

The nesting season for rooks is still some months ahead but their behaviour on a bright but gusty day showed that preliminaries are already beginning. Our local flock was using the wind to put on a show of aerobatics that seemed to owe a lot to high spirits. Pairs of birds were chasing each other in headlong dashes punctuated with sharp swerves and dives. Whether these were just flights of fancy or whether the birds were showing a serious interest in each other, I had no means of telling.

The rooks have also been congregating on the ground, not spread out as when feeding but in assemblies. As with the aerobatic displays these have the appearance of social occasions and there are signs of partners being chosen. Every now and then a cock rook starts to pay court to a hen.

A male rook in display is a fine sight. He may not have the colours and outrageous plumes of a peacock but he acquits himself well. His strutting is every bit as vigorous and stately. He holds his head high, droops his wings and paces towards the hen, spreading his tail in a surprisingly handsome fan as he bows and calls to her. Not even his black plumage is dull, it is shot with glossy green and purple in the autumn sunshine.

As the days shorten into winter, these displays will cease but they have laid the foundations for serious courtship in the rookeries as soon as the weather improves.

For a few weeks now, flocks of fieldfares and redwings have been patrolling the countryside. They are familiar immigrants from Scandinavia that appear every winter when that region is gripped in frost. The size and number of the flocks depend on conditions in these birds' native homes. Severe weather or failing food supplies set more on the move in the search for an easier life.

These are just some of the invaders that flee the harsher climate of northern and eastern Europe to spend part of the winter in the British Isles. The immigrants include flocks of starlings, lapwings and chaffinches, more spectacular short-eared owls and hen harriers, and a scattering of robins, tits and song thrushes. Even tiny goldcrests man-age the hazardous flight across the North Sea.

The newcomers blend in with residents of the same species and are not obvious as foreigners. An expert eye can see that continental blue tits are larger and brighter than the natives and will recognise that a flock of chaffinches in a field is foreign while individuals in the garden are more likely to be year-round residents.

If we have a cold spell, our own birds will be forced to move. Some head for the West Country and into Ireland, where the moderating influence of the Gulf Stream is stronger. Others head south to join human exiles in the winter resorts of France, Spain and Portugal.

DECEMBER

Ladybird

The ladybird was climbing the window but it fell off and lay on the sill with its legs waving helplessly. Before I could render assistance, it opened its wings, flipped into the air and landed right-way up. 'That was clever', I thought, but what happened next was much more intriguing. The wings were swung to the rear so they lay along the abdomen but extended well beyond the tip. And as I watched, they disappeared under the scarlet wingcases. It was as if they were being rolled up like a blind.

Insect wings lack the muscles that enable a bird or a bat to tuck its wings neatly against its body. So how did the ladybird fold its wings, reducing their area by about half, so they could fit under the wingcases?

When a ladybird, or any other beetle, swings its wings back from the extended flight position, they automatically start to buckle along preset-lines and they are folded into their final resting position by a simple mechanism. The abdomen raises slightly so that tiny brushes grip the wings, and then moves inwards, dragging the wings with it. The spikes detach, the abdomen extends again, rising to grip the wings further along their length and the cycle is repeated, until the folding is complete. The best analogy I can think of is the saw-edged feed-dogs that grip and pull material past the needle of a sewing machine. Not for the first time, I am impressed how nature has found the same solution to a problem as human ingenuity.

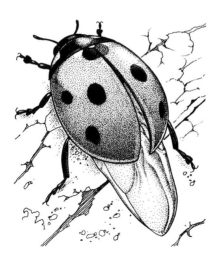

It was one of those brilliant autumn mornings. The mist had burned off leaving the atmosphere clear and cloudless and the microlights were buzzing overhead. At a lower level a flock of skylarks was flying to and fro. The larks would take off and disappear into the distance but they would soon be back, having circled at the far end of the field and flown back to where they started. All in all they gave the impression of being under the command of the Grand Old Duke of York. The characteristic loose and rather

erratic bounding flight that skylarks affect when flying in flocks added to the air of indecision.

At first, when the skylarks approached me out of a low sun, I had mistaken them for redwings, partly because of their thin 'seep' calls which are like the redwings' notes. The skylarks' calls have been called migration calls and it is very likely that this flock comprised birds which had come from northern and eastern Europe.

I had heard bursts of singing from early morning from the local birds and I had seen a few chases when individuals appeared to be trespassing. So, if the local birds were defending territories, as many birds do at this time of year, it seems more likely that the flock were visitors from far away. Continental skylarks enter this country while heading for southern Europe. The day was so warm that I was in shirtsleeves and the birds may have thought that they were already at their destination.

I can remember when fruit trees had sticky bands wrapped around their trunks. This was the traditional way to protect the foliage from attack by caterpillars of the winter moth. Insecticides now do the job more effectively. Sticky bands had to be applied long before the caterpillars hatched out because they were designed to trap the female moths when they were climbing the trunk to their egg-laying sites.

The female winter moth is unusual because her wings are rudimentary and she cannot fly. At some point in the winter she emerges from an underground pupa and walks towards the nearest vertical surface. In nature this will be a tree. On her way up the trunk she mates with a winged male, which is one of several kinds of moth that appear at lighted windows in winter. The female lays her eggs among lichens and mosses on the bark and on unopened buds. The eggs hatch in April and the caterpillars enter the buds and start devouring them. A heavy infestation of winter moths can defoliate a tree.

The oak has a natural defence against winter moths. Newly hatched caterpillars have to find buds which have just opened. They are not strong enough to penetrate closed buds and young leaves become too tough and indigestible within a few days. By varying the time when their leaves unfold, oak trees have a chance of foiling the young caterpillars and condemning them to starve to death. If this fails and the caterpillars do destroy the foliage, the oaks grow a replacement crop of leaves.

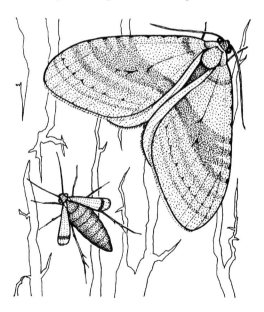

Keeping Warm

As you snuggle under the bedclothes on a cold night, spare a thought for the birds roosting outside. In fact, provided they retired with a good meal inside them, they should not be suffering. Their feathers act like our bedclothes and trap body heat. When a bird roosts, it fluffs out its feathers, increasing the amount of warm trapped air and giving greater insulation. At this time of

year they have the additional benefit of winter plumage which is thicker than the summer coat.

Even with good insulation, heat gradually leaks away and the body will chill unless there is a source of heat. Without a hot-water bottle or an electric blanket to supply extra heat, birds — like humans — begin to shiver. The muscles contract and relax rapidly without moving the limbs, like a motor car engine idling. Heat is generated and carried around the body by the blood. Birds shiver at intervals, depending on how cold they are. Shivering is not harmful, unless the body runs out of the food reserves needed to power the muscle contractions.

This is why birds need to be well-fed to survive the long winter nights. They convert the day's food into fat to see them through the hours of darkness, and some small birds also store extra food in the crop to digest through the night. Either way, the moral is to keep the birdtable stocked so the birds do not go to bed on an empty stomach.